Mike,

You are already AMAZING!
Your dad is certainly
proud of you guys.

Keep on looking up.

Your friend

Damare

DEDICATION

We dedicate this book to our Lord, Jesus Christ, in gratitude for His transformational saving grace. The privilege of receiving and passing on *The Articles of Transformation* is one of our life's greatest joys.

A special thank you to the love of our lives: our brilliant daughter, Giovannina. Thank you for your insights, love, and generosity in editing this book. May your tireless efforts be rewarded with God's anointing in every area of your life. You – our amazing girl – are a unique and creative soul.

Shine On!

Soli Deo Gloria!

The Articles of Transformation

by

Domenic Fusco, Ph.D.
Charlie Fusco, M.A.

The secret to life and the life to come!

What you hear, you think...
What you think, you believe...
What you believe, you become!

Contents

Hello Friend.

Are you longing to become the amazing person God has destined you to be? This book is for YOU!

Are you a young person facing the choices of college and career and about to take a leap into adulthood? This book is for YOU!

Have your dreams been crushed and failure has taken the wind out of your sails? This book is for YOU!

Do you feel lost and don't know how to go on? This book is for YOU!

PREFACE

Be Amazing! Learn how from the Ancient Olive Tree is the first subject covered in 𝔗he 𝒜rticles of 𝔗ransformation series. It has been created with the purpose of empowering people - just like YOU – by providing a format for an individualized personal discovery journey. It begins with questions only you can answer; and it guides you through transformational exercises - which when applied – will help you develop a strong foundation that will serve you all the days of your life.

The material in these pages (and on accompanying videos) offers revelatory inspirations that will launch you on the path to living out God's perfect plan for your life. (Jeremiah 29:11) No matter what lies behind you, the personal discovery journey ahead will serve to expand your vision, increase your understanding, and open your heart to receive the unique, prosperous, and *amazing* life intended for you alone.

Close observance of God's magnificent creation (as described in Romans 1:19-20), and personalizing the knowledge revealed and illustrated in these pages, lays the ground work for your transformational journey. The natural world will be your faithful tutor in developing the character attributes needed to advance and excel in every area of your life.

Understand: the *results of the self discovery journey will be equal to your participation.* Transformation beyond one's wildest dreams awaits any diligent seeker who is determined to lay hold of God's perfect plan for their life! Today is the day to step out of the shadows and become a shining light in the midst of the sea of mediocrity. *Be Amazing!*

INTRODUCTION

Have you ever reflected on the path that led you to where you are in life? When you think of tomorrow, next year, even your distant future, do you feel you are prepared? Or, are you just holding on to a hope and a prayer?

When arriving at one of life's cross-roads, one direction can lead to an exciting opportunity while the other choice can lead us spiraling down the proverbial rabbit hole. The big "unknowns" can take us on an emotional roller coaster ride. But, take heart! Within the pages to come, you will find answers to so many of those "unknowns"; and you will be equipped to confidently "go for the gold"!

When I was seventeen and finishing high school, I had big dreams. I imagined myself traveling the world and making lots of money. But, those thoughts of living the "high life" as we called it back in the day were mere daydreams. Not only didn't I have a specific plan as to how I could actually achieve those goals, I had no plan at all. I was just "happening". I was direction-less, without parental or other guidance, with no advocate in my corner, and no money to boot. My **dreams** were just that: momentarily flights of fancy to help me flee my uncomfortable reality. They were a mental exercise that helped me escape the painful and mundane life I witnessed all around me. Those daydreams were merely castles built on sand; and yet, I embraced the aspirations of "the good life" that danced in my head. I hoped they would come true: but how? I had no clue. Do you?

My lack of knowledge as to how to build the life of my dreams, as well as my lack of trust-worthy guidance, left me ill-prepared to find true prosperity of mind, body, soul, and spirit. Finding my way in life, via education, career-choice or personal pursuits, was strictly a roll of the dice. But, by the magnificent GRACE of GOD, my once downward spiral transformed into a stairway to unending heights of dreams come true. I have happily arrived here - nearly fifty years later - determined to save those struggling with the big unknowns from the pitfalls and utter destitution of a life without vision that I once knew. That brings us to the *vision-maker message* found in the pages to come.

To make the point clear, I want to differentiate the definitions between the words **dream** and **vision**.

In part, Google Dictionary defines **Dream** like this:
1. Cherished aspiration, ambition, or ideal
Example: *"I fulfilled a childhood dream when I became champion"*
Synonyms: ambition, aspiration, hope.
2. (To) indulge in daydreams or fantasies about something greatly desired.
Example: *"She had dreamed of a trip to Italy"*

Merriam-Webster: takes the definition of **dream** a step further:
1. A state of mind marked by abstraction or release from reality.

That's where I found myself at seventeen.

Vision is conceptually very different from a dream! Google Dictionary offers clarity on the subject as follows:
1. The ability to think about or plan the future with imagination or wisdom.

Synonyms: imagination, creativity, creative power, inventiveness, innovation, inspiration, intuition, perceptiveness, perception, breadth of view, foresight, insight, far-sightedness, prescience, discernment, awareness, penetration, shrewdness, sharpness, cleverness.

Although some dictionaries define vision and dream as somewhat similar, I find the definitions provided here contrast the two concepts distinctly for our purposes.

We define dream versus vision as follows:

> **A dream is marked by a release from reality while vision shows a mindful, intentional deliberation, and co-operation between creativity and wisdom which results in the success of a far-sighted plan.**
>
> Domenic and Charlie Fusco

A visionary holds onto an exact goal or plan for the future, and sees it to completion, by "breadth of view", "sharpness", "innovation" and "inspiration".

Dreams of the imagination are easily forgotten; yet a true vision is an ever-motivating life force! No matter what hardship, challenge or delay you may encounter, vision remains. It will propel you toward a goal by fueling you with hope, faith, and the clarity of mind to order your steps in the way necessary to achieve your goals. A fully formed vision burns within you as you awake each day calling you onward and upward. It becomes your delightful daily bread.

Find an achiever and you'll find a person of **vision**. Vision is an intrinsic character trait found in all who achieve great success. Consider King David who was transformed from a simple shepherd boy and creative, free spirit into a giant slayer who led victorious armies. He became a beloved king who founded a permanent dynasty through his **vision** to unite the twelve tribes of Israel. Another spiritual luminary was tiny Mother Teresa of Calcutta whose vision to show mercy and love to the poorest of the poor is a living legacy carried on by those she tutored through her acts of compassion.

From the inventive, breadth of view expressed through the brilliant mind of Einstein to the intuition, and far-sightedness to plan for the future of a skyline or a country found in Donald Trump, **VISION** is the common fuel and sustaining force that culminates in realized goals. Whether a vision is God breathed or self- born, a person with an unshakable vision will experience remarkable achievement in the midst of the floundering and fearful masses. **Vision** is the special enabler of an over-coming, victorious mindset that separates victors from victims.

To begin your transformational journey, it is strategic that you are armed with the message of Jeremiah 29:11.

> *For I know the plans I have for you, declares the LORD, plans to prosper you and not to harm you, plans to give you hope and a future.*

Be discerning as you consider the depth of understanding you may gain from the first phrase of this passage: "For I know the plans I have for you". And who is making this declaration? None other than God!

Jeremiah 29"11 makes this clear: the promise of a hopeful future is not in the plans you have for yourself. It informs the reader that the plan for your life is not just "a plan". The Lord of Heaven spells it out loud and clear. He has a singular, unique plan to prosper you and not harm you: a future filled with hope! How cool is that?

The Christian who takes their faith seriously understands that God is a loving Father who wants to be intimately involved in every aspect of His child's life: "if" and "when" He is welcomed to do so. You are not a puppet. You were created to be a free agent. You can choose to go it alone. The Lord will never force you to accept or embrace His will or His plan for your life. But, wisdom calls you to consider His higher way.

The beginning step on your transformational journey is to invite your Heavenly Father to become your guide. Seeking to know and follow His perfect plan leads to a life of grace and favor.

> *"Are you tired? Worn out? Burned out on religion? Come to me. Get away with me and you'll recover your life. I'll show you how to take a real rest. Walk with me and work with me—watch how I do it. Learn the unforced rhythms of grace. I won't lay anything heavy or ill-fitting on you. Keep company with me and you'll learn to live freely and lightly."*
> Matthew 11:28-30 The Message

Today, you are being offered deliverance from the pitfalls experienced by unbelievers or nominal Christians who develop their life plan with little or no thought to *the plan* that leads to true prosperity of mind, body, spirit and soul. Take this message to heart and lay hold of *the plan* which promises a safe and hopeful future under the care of the God who loves you.

That is what The Articles of Transformation are all about. The books and videos have been created to get you on the path to discovering who God is, who you are, who you want to be, and God's unique plan for your life. The practical exercises you will complete at the end of each chapter address the "what" and the "why" in your personal discovery journey. These exercises aid in the character development that is essential in becoming all you are destined to be.

The Articles of Transformation's self discovery process is, above all things, a spiritual eye-opener. It causes you to see yourself as the whole child of God you were created to be: spirit, soul, mind, and body. We trust the knowledge and character attributes you will glean from **The Olive Tree** will flood the path before you with God's transformational grace, light, and love.

Get ready to step into God's prosperous blueprint for your life! Now is the moment in time when you begin the process of discovering **AMAZING YOU!**

Godspeed on your transformational journey!

Domenic and Charlie Fusco

We, of course, have plenty of wisdom to pass on to you once you get your feet on firm spiritual ground, but it's not popular wisdom, the fashionable wisdom of high-priced experts that will be out-of-date in a year or so. God's wisdom is something mysterious that goes deep into the interior of his purposes. You don't find it lying around on the surface. It's not the latest message, but more like the oldest—what God determined as the way to bring out His best in us, long before we ever arrived on the scene. The experts of our day haven't a clue about what this eternal plan is. If they had, they wouldn't have killed the Master of the God-designed life on a cross. That's why we have this Scripture text: No one's ever seen or heard anything like this, Never so much as imagined anything quite like it— What God has arranged for those who love him. But you've seen and heard it because God by his Spirit has brought it all out into the open before you.

1 Corinthians 2:9

The Message

17

View the two minute film on the origin of the Articles at:
http://articlesoftransformation.com/beamazing

PROLOGUE

The story of The Articles of Transformation begins with a boy
who grew up in the latter part of the 19th century. As a member of a
poor family who were pawns of the Industrial Revolution, this young
lad became discontent with his station in life. By his early twenties,
he set out to find the distant paradise he increasingly longed for.
As the story goes, after recovering five weeks from a death defying
fall in the remote mountains of the Himalayans, and being cared for
by an old man, The Articles of Transformation were handed to the
young lad in a leather folder which had been artistically tooled with
great detail. The old mentor spoke these words:

In this folder is the prized possession of my life:
The Articles of Transformation.
Read them aloud and often;
for these words will become your thoughts...
your thoughts will become your beliefs...
and these beliefs will empower your actions.
If you are faithful to do this, you will realize
great wealth, success, and true peace.

The Articles have been passed down from one chosen person to
another for centuries. I received them in 1977 and have decided to
share them with you.

CHAPTER ONE

Reach Higher

Poet Maya Angelou penned this admonition: If you get, give. If you learn, teach. As one who has been given the greatest of gifts, I now pass it on to you. What I have learned … am learning… I teach that we all may grow to our potential and be a blessings in this world. I invite you to take advantage of the insights for transformation found within this study of creation's wonders and wish you Godspeed as you begin your journey into infinite possibilities. I encourage you to allow the words and exercises presented in this book to ignite a spark within you… a spark of transformation which will guide you into all truth. Those who have taken this journey before you… those who journey now… are in your corner encouraging you to take this leap of destiny.

Before you move on to the unraveling of ancient mysteries, I would like to tell you the inspirational story of someone whose life is a sterling illustration of what can happen as you grasp the essence of even one principle found in 𝔗he 𝒜rticles of 𝔗ransformation. The transformational path taken by a young woman I met while filming a documentary in the middle of Siberia is not unlike the journey which lies before you.

Our plane landed in Ulan Ude as temperatures plummeted to minus forty-five degrees. Also known as "the Secret City", Ulan Ude didn't appear on U.S.S.R. maps for many decades. It was home to the Soviet Union's largest and most top-secret military installation. Although a few years had passed since the end of the Cold War with the United States, and we Americans were no longer considered by them to be "the evil empire", the old Soviet guard (made up of hard core communists or socialists at best) was still in charge. They had changed their outward appearance from "comrade attire"; but, their thinking was still imprisoned in the controlling ideology of communism as were the people under their influence.

My short stay in Ulan Ude made me acutely aware of my many blessings back home in sunny Florida. As we disembarked the plane, ice, snow, and the bitter cold of Siberia's long, dark winter days greeted us. It was a rude awakening. The cold took your breath away; muscles would tremble and spasm. Even a drip from your nose became an instant icicle.

When we arrived at our host's humble apartment, it became clear that it lacked the storage space for all our filming gear or enough sleeping accommodations for the entire crew. I volunteered to split-up from the group and move to other lodging. No! I didn't get a room at a Holiday Inn. My move was to a tiny apartment shared by three missionaries.

Upon arrival at my new digs, I was shown to my bed of sorts: an ancient, dingy sofa with no pillow. But, I was tired and grateful to have a warm place to rest my head. Like all the other apartments and homes in Ulan Ude, our heat was delivered from a single source at the outskirts of the city. If the generator went out, there would be no heat or hot water. So, safe from the frigid cold beyond the door,

I settled in and said a fervent prayer for that energy station to "keep on keeping on".

It was at that apartment that I met Vicka. The only table in the apartment seated just three people. On one occasion when it was my turn to take a seat, I was joined by Vicka. Of the three roommates, she was the only one who could speak English. Set before us was the most basic of meals: a crust of bread, yogurt, a bit of soup, and weak coffee. Coffee was a precious commodity. Just enough was used to flavor the hot water. There were no sodas, no sugar, no snacks, no Starbucks. Every part of the lifestyle was a study in limitations.

At the end of a day of filming, there was little else to do than linger over dinner and chat. Vicka and I engaged in a lengthy conversation. I listened intently as in her broken English she revealed her deep discontent. She felt trapped and limited. She was searching for more from life. Like so many others around the world, she longed for the kind of life we often take for granted in the West.

During our warm cultural and philosophical exchange, I asked Vicka what she really would love to do in life. She paused briefly, and then said timidly, "One day I would love to see Moscow… just once in my life!" Her body language and down-cast eyes indicated she thought her dream was quite impossible. The conditions and controls put in place by the past political state were mentally limiting her possibilities for the future.

Remote and unchanged by the new and growing freedoms being experienced by others across Russia, Ulan Ude's people were frozen in time. Their lives were diminished by lack of knowledge. I'm not speaking of education: for their population have more folks with doctorates than almost anywhere other people group on the globe. I am discussing "lack of knowledge" in the sense that they didn't know the truth about their purpose and God's plan for their lives.

My people are destroyed for lack of knowledge.

Hosea 4:6   NASB

I began to encourage Vicka to dream. I painted a picture of freedom in her mind with positive words. Much like Jim Rohn had spoken into my life so many years before, I began to share principles that would help Vicka change her don'ts to do's. I caught her up to speed on how things were rapidly changing for the better in Russia. I assured her that her dream of visiting Moscow – only five hours away by plane - was not only possible but probable. I could see the light of hope in her eyes. Evening was spent. I ended our time of sharing with these words:

... with God all things are possible.

Matthew 19:26

New International Version

That day in Ulan Ude was one of thousands of conversations I've had throughout my life. But for Vicka... it was "the one" that would change her life forever!

A few days later, I was approached by an elder in Ulan Ude's religious community. He began to scream at me: "Don't tell these youngsters any of your foolishness. It's false hope. They'll be even more disappointed than ever when they never get to see Moscow. Don't encourage them. They will learn to cope with their place in life here." I held my tongue out of respect for this man's position as their local spiritual leadership; however, I knew he was wrong and far from knowing my God of infinite possibilities. But, it wasn't my turf… not my call. I had done what I could. I went on my way without further contact with Vicka trusting that a seed of faith planted in a fertile soul would blossom.

Five years passed. I was shocked when I received a surprise phone call from Vicka. Not only had she been to Moscow, she was calling from Ireland where she had been employed for almost a year. You see, Vicka had learned how to move the immovable. She refused to give up on her vision. And better still, she didn't stop there. She began to dream even bigger dreams. The last time I received a call from Vicka, she was in Myrtle Beach, South Carolina. She had been in the States for over a month. That young woman's vision to see the world defied the presence of naysayers. She refused to be discouraged by those who couldn't envision anything but the mundane life she had escaped from three thousand miles away. Now the warm sun of her dreams were kissing her face.

Everything is possible to the one who believes.
Mark 9:23
HCSB

Opportunities and advantages don't assure us success in life. Limitations and struggles can't keep us from achieving success. Success… true success… comes from the character we possess within. It is rooted in where we place our faith and confidence.

Character is a widely under-developed, elusive, and an under-rated source of power in today's culture. Character development is so important that I am including its definition from Webster's Dictionary. It is paramount that "the why" it's so essential to success is not lost on those who engage in this study. The character lessons and exercises you are about to encounter in a thorough perusal of 𝔖he 𝒜rticles of 𝔖ransformation are foundation blocks for building the life of your dreams. They are urgently critical to grasp at this time in history.

Look to Webster's Dictionary for the definition of character:
> **2c: the complex of mental and ethical traits marking and often individualizing a person, group, or nation**

Simply defined, character is the psychological pattern of your mental and ethical traits. These traits determine how you will instinctively act and react in given situations. It is how you are programmed… wired if you will… and how you are motivated. Your character is essentially what you think and believe, and consequently, how you will act when you are put to test.

Booker T. Washington is noted for saying: *Character is Power.* Make no mistake: every true success story or failure in life has to do with character or the lack thereof.
- Character is the essence of who you are.
- Character is made up of the core principles that govern your life.
- Character cannot be bought. Character is built! Character is power. It produces true success.

The process of building character begins with:
What you hear, YOU think.
What you think, YOU believe.
What you believe, YOU become!

Let's examine closely what sparked Vicka's transformational journey. Do you remember that I asked her to tell me what she really wanted to do in life? That's the way transformation begins. You have to get real about who you are… what you desire deep down in your heart… and you must dare to say it to yourself. You have to own your vision. After Vicka dared to speak of her secret wish, something changed. She set heaven in motion to work on her behalf to bring it to pass.

> *Be delighted with the Lord. Then he will give you all your heart's desires. Commit everything you do to the Lord. Trust him to help you do it, and he will.*
>
> Psalms 37:4-5
>
> Living Bible (TLB)

As Vicka affirmed her vision with her own voice; those words became her thoughts… her "prayer without ceasing". Her thoughts became her beliefs; and, her beliefs became her experiences. Once Vicka stepped out of her box of limitations, she never looked back. So, you may ask, "Where is Vicka now?" Happily I can report that she is pursuing her passion. Vicka's story is an amazing chronicle of personal transformation. Today, she makes her home, and teaches English, in her beloved Moscow.

Vicka's story is not much different than yours and mine. When her transformational journey began she had issues… circumstances… relationships… that held her back from who she was destined to be. Perhaps that's you right now; but it doesn't have to be you tomorrow! The mysteries held within the *Articles of Transformation* call you to a higher life. Take my hand. Allow me the honor of being your guide on this exciting journey. Let's cross the finish line together!

The Olive Tree
Vision

*P*rosperous is the one who understands that a life without vision is utterly destitute. For with vision, seemingly unattainable treasures will become his legacy.

CHAPTER TWO

The Ancient Olive Tree

If you recall from the Prologue *The Articles of Transformation* were handed to the young lad in a leather folder which had been artistically tooled with great detail. The old man spoke these words:

In this folder is the prized possession of my life: seven articles, The Articles of Transformation. Read them aloud and often; for these words will become your thoughts... your thoughts will become your beliefs... and these beliefs will empower your actions. If you are faithful to do this, you will realize great wealth, success, and true peace.

Read the words of the first of seven articles, *The Ancient Olive Tree*, on the next page and see if you can unravel some of the secrets of God's power and divinity He has encapsulated in the olive tree and are hidden in plain sight for us to understand the character attribute of vision.

Prosperous is the one who understands that a life without vision is utterly destitute. For with vision, seemingly unattainable treasures will become his legacy.

Held captive in the lost history of ancient days are secrets which may only be discovered in the revelations of the distant future. For we know that after the cleansing of the earth when all living things were covered by water, that those who were spared sent out a raven, then a dove, in search of a sign of life. Hope for a restored earth and a future filled with promise was renewed when the dove returned bearing an olive branch. What unknown strength and fortitude did the ancient olive tree possess? How did it survive such cataclysmic destruction and live to blossom and bear fruit once again? What wondrous secret does the olive tree hold for the curious of soul?

In planning an olive grove, one must count the cost; for the olive tree grows with great patience enduring the changes and chances of Nature for longer than a thousand years. The one who plants might never behold a mature crop seeing that a span of fifty years or more may be required for a full harvest to occur. For many who toil in the orchard, their children's children will reap the benefits of their life's work.

The planting of the olive grove must be carried out with regard to the requirements of individual trees. Each tree should be separated from the others by a length of thirty strides. The despised enemy of the olive tree is the olive fly. It breeds, not in the tree's wood which is resistant to decay, but in the flesh of the fruit. The olive tree is most susceptible to the olive fly when deprived of water. When poorly nourished, the crop will become erratic, bearing a heavy crop one year and putting forth not even a blossom the next.

Pruning is a highly judicious art. It protects the health of the tree by permitting greater circulation of air; for the olive tree is wind pollinated. The cutting away of live branches may seem foolish, even wasteful, when assessing the tree's abundant productivity in past seasons. Yet, this severe act will revitalize an aged tree, compensate for root loss, and promote desirable blossom formation for the coming season. The master pruner must know the individual needs of each tree in the grove. With the exactness of a sculptor's skillful hand, he prunes each specimen taking into consideration the tree's age, health, limb support and penetration of sunlight. That which appears destitute in the fall will surely prosper for years to come through the master pruner's acts of vision.

What wisdom requires the olive tree to experience the cold and chilling winter in order to blossom and bring forth fruit in season? Although many fruit trees require either much or little water to flourish, the olive tree will tolerate six months of drought followed by an abundance of water without destructive consequence. Desirable olives do not come from seedlings; they come from grafting branches of unquestionable quality into young trees which have shown themselves strong.

Harvesters look forward to the well-earned reward of their diligent planning, planting, and pruning. When autumn delivers fruit in shades of deep green to a straw yellow or cherry red, harvesting begins. Without fail, the fruit must be gathered before it turns black and before the frost can halt its peak perfection. One cannot help but reflect on the past year when there was little rain and much concern. Yet, the dreams of those who planned, planted and pruned have brought forth a bountiful yield.

The fruit you hold in your hand is not your own. It is the legacy of the hands that tended the trees in expectation for generations before you. The many trees you nurture without reward of harvest will yield their fruitfulness to the cultivators who follow in your path. Without vision, and the faith of those who worked for things they could not see, you would be without a harvest. And, should you the care-taker of today cease to dream, would not the Future's children be deprived of the priceless gifts and secrets of the wise and ancient olive tree?

Download your FREE artistic poster at http://eepurl.com/ggTGgT

It has taken me decades to understand the many layers of insight in each nature study. And now the door to these mysteries is opened to you with the key. Your journey to find hidden treasures begins with the revelation of how our vision for God's plan for our life is tied to all those who come after us.

The Olive Tree contains timeless truths about the character principle of **VISION**: how it can be practically applied and bring immediate and long-term results to your life. The simplest way to communicate the meaning of this article is through the acronym OLIVE. Each letter represents a positive step in the direction of your transformed life. The first letter of our acronym OLIVE is "**O**" for Old. Consider the following words from The Olive Tree.

> In planning an olive grove, one must count the cost; for the olive tree grows with great patience enduring the changes and chances of Nature for longer than a thousand years. The one who plants might never behold a mature crop seeing that a span of fifty years or more may be required for a full harvest to occur. For many who toil in the orchard, their children's children will reap the benefits of their life's work.

While meditating on this article, perhaps - like me – you began to view this allegorical piece as a treasure hunt. I began to think about how the olive tree related to my future.

Like the one planning to plant the olive grove, we must be faithful to do all within our ability to insure the crop to come. That raises other important considerations.

- What must I do to realize my potential and maximize the time allotted to me?
- What are the most important things I want to accomplish?
- How does *The Olive Tree* relate to my need for character transformation, my productivity, and security in my old age?
- How do I discover God's plan for my life?

We begin this study by looking forward. The first letter "O" of the acronym OLIVE represents OLD.

Write today's date here:

_____

Consider the date ten years from today and write it on the following line:

_____ .

Now, write as large as you can how OLD you will be 10 years from today in the space on the next page.

How OLD you will be 10 years from today.
Write it below as LARGE as you can.

Most people are shocked to actually view their number ten years from today in black and white. Purpose to make each of those days count!

THE VIRTUE OF PATIENCE

The planter of olive trees cannot expect fruit for some time. He must be forward-looking knowing that the luscious fruit will not have its first showing for as many as seven years. A well-maintained olive tree can require as long as twenty years to produce a mature crop while an olive tree which receives inadequate care may struggle for as many as fifty years to produce a mature crop. The grower persists in giving care to branches covered only with leaves year after year because he knows his efforts will establish an olive tree whose life expectancy and productivity can exceed more than a thousand years.

The olive tree grower's hope for a successful harvest is rooted in the exercise of patience. Jokingly, I've heard people say it took them "twenty years to become an overnight success". Many of us can identify with this and given the chance, we might wish to skip certain growth requirements and jump ahead to the goal post. What the olive tree teaches us is that we should never settle for a short term gain at the expense of a long term goal: a mature crop. Although you live in the moment, you must be equally attentive to planning and planting for future success.

 Did you have goals you wanted to accomplish over the past ten years? What did you achieve? Where did you fail? Planning is not only prudent; but imperative.

He who fails to plan is planning to fail!

The quote above - attributed to a wide variety of highly successful individuals from Benjamin Franklin to Winston Churchill and widely used by contemporary self-help gurus - is not to be taken lightly. All of these men were on to something!

At this time, move to the following ***Personal Discovery Exercise***. Complete Personal Discovery Exercise. Add Personal Reflections to the journaling section before proceeding to 𝔗he 𝒜rticles of 𝔗ransformation.

The Articles of Transformation **Personal Discovery Exercise**

To further develop the character attribute of vision, answer these questions:

How old will your loved ones be in 10 years? Where will they be? Use the space below to write their names and your projected vision of them in 10 years. (i.e. parents, siblings, spouse, mentors, close friends, etc)

Relationship	How Old Will they Be?	Where will they be?

What are you thinking now?

Sobering exercise, isn't it?

To exercise the character attribute of Vision further look to the years ahead and consider the purpose of your life. What will be said of you when your time comes? What will people think about your life?

Write your obituary in the space provided. Reflect on it and decide "Is this how I want to be remembered?"

Most memorials are limited to one or two lines to sum up an entire life. What would you hope yours would be?

What will be written on your tombstone?

What must you do to be that person? List the goals you must accomplish to deserve that remembrance:

You have just accomplished an exercise only a few people every perform in their lives. You have taken the first step in becoming amazing!

Reinforce your experience and learning by viewing the artistic video for lesson 2 at:

https://www.articlesoftransformation.com/beamazing/

Be Amazing...

Let Him open your eyes and
you will see amazing things ahead.

John 9:30   HCS Bible

CHAPTER THREE

Olive Tree: List Your Goals

The second letter of our acronym **OLIVE** is **L** for **LIST.**

YOU ARE GOD'S UNIQUE CREATION

The planting of the olive grove must be carried out with regard to the requirements of individual trees. Each tree should be separated from the others by a length of thirty strides.

Scripture tells us that we are unique creations of God.

Thank you for making me so wonderfully complex! It is amazing to think about. Your workmanship is marvelous—and how well I know it.

Psalms 139:14
Living Bible

Job 37:7 (New American Standard Bible) reveals that each of us is uniquely marked by the unlimited creativity of God.

He seals the hand of every man, that all men may know his work.

Our fingerprints leave an image of our individuality on everything we touch. Even "identical" twins receive distinct fingerprints. Their outward appearance may look the same to others, but God has given each of them – each of us - divine identity and purpose shared by no other.

Just as olives trees are separated by distance for proper growth to occur and to allow their individual traits to be observed and cared for, you must realize you are unlike every other person and have special requirements for optimum growth. You, too, require time and room to grow as an individual without a constant barrage of external influence or distractions from others in the grove of your life.

The real person God has purposed you to become is realized through knowledge of Him and developing an intimate relationship with Him. Your individual potential is known by God alone. He made you to be fruitful as you deeply plant your roots in His kingdom. Embrace your uniqueness; and ask God to begin fully forming you from the inside out. Dr. Robert H. Schuller sums it up this way:

> *Any man can count the seeds in an apple, but only God can count the apples in a seed.*

Pray and ask God for direction. List Your Goals-re-visit them. Write down your goals in a private and permanent journal. The Personal Discovery Journal was created to help you "record your vision" and stay on course. Begin to develop plans to accomplish your vision.

Then the Lord answered me and said, "Record the vision and inscribe

it on tablets, that the one who reads it may run. " For the vision is yet for the appointed time; it hastens toward the goal, and it will not fail. Though it tarries, wait for it; for it will certainly come, it will not delay.

Habakkuk 2:2-3

New American Standard Bible

If you do not record your goals, then you have the liberty of conveniently changing direction or forgetting them. This is the difference between "pie in the sky" and vision. A true vision never seems to leave you alone. It is persistent. If your goal is really important to you, write it down!

As you begin to write down your goals, it is essential that you be totally honest with yourself. After all, you are the only one privy to your hidden desires and dreams. Do not solicit other people's opinions, lest you fall prey to copying someone else's blueprint for life. What may be a calling for one person could very well be imprisonment for another.

Clarifying your vision and goals may seem a difficult task initially. You may have stifled your dreams so long or have been enveloped in the dreams of another to the extent that you're not in touch with your goals on a conscious level. You may need to "dig deep" to unleash your visionary abilities. Just as any athletic ability is developed through repeated exercises to develop strength and skill, your vision muscle will strengthen by reason of use.

Realizing your dreams starts by a simple act of writing down your goals one by one. Most people take weeks, months, even years to determine their life plan: the practical 1, 2, 3 - A, B, C steps required to get to their "happy ending".

Reflect on the olive tree for inspiration. It doesn't produce a full crop for years but it stands the test of time. Exercise patience knowing that your life is a sacred design of God. The dreams, goals, and visions He has placed within you should be nurtured as a sacred trust.

> *For I know the plans I have for you, says the Lord. They are plans for good and not for evil, to give you a future and a hope.*
>
> Jeremiah 29:11
>
> Living Bible

God's empowerment to achieve your goals is not "a given". Becoming a true partner with God may require you to make significant changes. It is not enough to be "spiritual" or "religious" as is a commonly held cultural belief today. The God of the Bible is not "lousy-goosey" about His expectations for us. He has given us high directives for patterning our lives after the virtues modeled before us in the life of His Son, Jesus Christ.

You cannot expect God's blessing to comply with an uninformed understanding of His benevolence... or your rules. He's the One who directs. He is a loving Father! You can easily discover if you're living outside of the guidelines for His participation in your success. The more you read Scripture, the clearer His new covenant with you will become. Talk to Him naturally as a child would talk to His father.

God doesn't ask you to guess how to please Him; He has outlined his requirements specifically in His Word. Living in willful disobedience (sin) limits His blessings. Pray for God's help and guidance. Be open to His correction. Have confidence in His goodness. Choose wisely the path to true success.

And this is the confidence (the assurance, the privilege of boldness) which we have in Him: [we are sure] that if we ask anything (make any request) <u>according to His will</u> (in agreement with His own plan), He listens to and hears us. And if (since) we [positively] know that He listens to us in whatever we ask, we also know [with settled and absolute knowledge] that we have [granted us as our present possessions] the requests made of Him.

1 John 5:14-15

Amplified Bible

A petition is a form of prayer. In our governmental affairs, a formal petition is made to a higher power to obtain their support such as petitioning a governor for a pardon using the standing law to support the granting of the request. As God is the supreme higher power, we should approach him with at least the same preparedness that we would an earthly authority.

This is how writing down your goals can best work for you. Formally make a "prayer of petition" for God's intervention in your life. Ask Him to work through you to bring your vision to pass within the confines of what Scripture promises He WILL DO and WILL PROVIDE for His children. Your petition acts as a willful invitation to your Heavenly Father and His angels to come to your aid and to watch over His Word to perform it on your behalf.

I want to make a clear distinction between what is being related through The Articles of Transformation as compared to certain New Age or self-help teachings. We do not ascribe to the non-biblical theory that we receive a response to our written goals from "the universe" or "the law of attraction". In truth, we receive cooperation to see our visions realized from the living God who created the universe! There is a very great gulf of separation in partnering with a personal God who loves you than with an unknowable force.

The distinct difference between the Articles and most self-help teachings is self-help puts you at the center of your life, your vision, goals, decisions and even disciplines. The Articles put God at the center of your life: His vision, will, and disciplines for your success.

DEVELOP THE HABIT OF GOAL SETTING

A Harvard study revealed that in one graduating class only 3% of the graduates developed the habit of writing down goals. Near the end of their careers, an amazing thing had happened. The 3% who made goals and wrote them down were not only more successful, but had assets greater than the remaining 97% of the graduating class combined! Today you join an elite group: those who know the secret to a successful future.

Continue to make a List of Your Goals on the following pages.
- Daily
- Weekly
- Quarterly
- Yearly
- Five year
- Ten year
- Life-long

Highlight the EASILY ACHIEVABLE GOALS to help you develop a winning and hopeful attitude. Begin with a simple grocery list or a "fix-it" list. List goals which can realistically and that can easily be accomplished this week.

Question: "How do you eat an elephant?" Answer: "ONE bite at a time." That's how you go about goal setting. Start small and expand as you conquer a few short term goals.

Do not get caught up in so much detail and such long-term thinking that you suffer paralysis from over-analysis. The more items you check off your list, the more successful you will feel… the more confident you will become. Success begets success!

> **Hope deferred makes the heart sick, but desire fulfilled is a tree of life.**

Proverbs 13:12
New American Standard Bible

At this time, complete the following Personal Discovery Journal Exercise before proceeding to the next chapter of The Articles of Transformation.

The Articles of Transformation **Personal Discovery Exercise**

Make a love list… wish list… want to achieve list… I will be list.
List physical items you wish to acquire, career goals, spiritual and
personal transformation you desire.

*The ultimate exercise includes two factors: your personal wants and
desires for the future and beginning to understand what God's plan
is for your future. It's a process to discover both. You will have a much
better understanding after you have completed the next section.*

TEN YEAR GOALS:
Spiritual goals:

_____

_____

_____

_____

_____

_____

Material goals:

_____

_____

_____

_____

_____

_____

_____

_____

Career goals:

_____

_____

_____

_____

_____

_____

Personal transformation goals:

_____

_____

_____

_____

_____

Other goals:

_____

_____

_____

_____

_____

Once you have written down your goals, dwell on them and then order them in order of importance in your permanent journal. Most people who have never done this exercise (95% of you) will take a while to look at them and adjust them. Very often it takes as long as a year to clarify your true God given goals.

TENDING YOUR OLIVE TREE

By now you should have listed your ten year goals (in this book). Return to those pages and evaluate each item. Determine what is really most important to you. Remove goals that belong to other people or were motivated by others. Discard goals that do not represent your deeply held heart's desires or those that are incompatible with your Christian faith. Meditate on the course you have chosen. Refine your lists to reflect clarity of vision.

Setting Goals is a habit you should exercise throughout your entire life. Don't wait until year's end to set goals for the year. Begin today. You do not need to make "New Year's Resolutions" if you are already resolved in your life's direction.

Now that you have set your personal goals (spirit, soul and body), begin to evaluate how the goals of those around you affect you and how yours affect them. If the goals of others negatively change your focus or drive you away from your Godly goals, you must address the conflict - no matter how painful. This can include family relationships, employers, friends and more. Obligations are upon us all. Seek God's help to find peaceful resolutions with conflicting life visions.

At times you will need to alter your method or your time-line for achieving your desired goals because of unrealistic time allowances or unexpected emergencies. Whatever comes your way, get back on track by reviewing your written goals often and remapping the steps to achieve them. Don't Stop! If you falter, start again immediately with greater resolve. The reward is worth the journey!

Therefore, since we are surrounded by such a huge crowd of witnesses to the life of faith, let us strip off every weight that slows us down, especially the sin that so easily trips us up. And let us run with endurance the race God has set before us. We do this by keeping our eyes on Jesus, the champion who initiates and perfects our faith. Because of the joy awaiting him, he endured the cross, disregarding its shame. Now he is seated in the place of honor beside God's throne. Think of all the hostility he endured from sinful people; then you won't become weary and give up.

Hebrews 12: 1-3

New Living Translation

Revisit the pages of your Personal Discovery Journal often to stay on track and evaluate your progress. You will shortly discover the difference between a whim (fantasy) and heart-felt vision (goal). Remove from your list items that are short lived. Use your journal pages to flesh out the goals that you wish to ignite.

PRIVACY SETTING ALERT

Today it seems as if our culture is besieged with "over-share". From talk shows to awards shows and social media there is little that is held as private. Your goals are PRIVATE. Be judicious in where and with whom you share them; sharing them broadly may bring unwelcome results.

Many people confuse mentoring and accountability with their facebook "friends" list. Celebrate your victories, no matter how small, broadly if you wish. But, reserve sharing your crosses with your confessor, mentor, pastor, counselor, or mental health professional. Whoever you choose to confide in should be worthy of your confidence and your dreams. Be selective.

BE RESOLUTE

No matter what you encounter in your journey, remain true to your vision despite apparent setbacks. Look once more to the wisdom of **The Olive Tree.**

TRANSFORMATIONAL ENEMIES

The despised enemy of the olive tree is the olive fly. It breeds, not in the tree's wood which is resistant to decay, but in the flesh of the fruit.

Just when you start to see fruitfulness in your life, certain "enemies" come and try and steal your yield. Perhaps the old enemy of self-doubt starts eating away at you. Distracting, discouraging thoughts cross your mind saying you won't be able to sustain momentum… you don't have what it takes… you're not good enough. See your enemy for who he is.

> ***A thief comes only to steal and to kill and to destroy. I have come so that they may have life and have it in abundance.***
>
> John 10:10
>
> HCSB

Be discriminating about sharing your goals; reserve them for yourself. Your Personal Discovery Journal is just that: PERSONAL. Prematurely sharing your dreams and personal reflections with even those closest to you may bring unexpected reactions.

Certainly your thought-life needs to be reigned-in when it gets off track with God's promises for your success. God gives instructions and tools for accomplishing that. Bringing down the enemies within is entirely within your control.

We use our powerful God-tools for smashing warped philosophies, tearing down barriers erected against the truth of God, fitting every loose thought and emotion and impulse into the structure of life shaped by Christ. Our tools are ready at hand for clearing the ground of every obstruction and building lives of obedience into maturity.

2 Corinthians 10:5

The Message

Enemies from without are far more trying to deal with than ones self-born. Who are these enemies? Most often, your enemies come from your close circle: family and friends. As you become increasingly productive and make noticeable changes in your direction, your inner circle might perceive that they have something to lose.

We often expect our families and friends will have our backs and cheer us onward only to find they are threatened, even angry, if we express that we are somehow unhappy with our present state. Many of those who have shared your old life found it a comforting place for them. They may take it personally or even be fearful about how your change of direction will affect your relationship with them. They may fear being left behind or fear your expectations of them will change as you pursue your vision. Unfortunately, insecurity, fear of loss, fear of the unknown, even just the word change can bring negative reactions to the new olives on your branches. Although "attacks on your fruit" may not be deliberate or done out of any contempt for you, you may find your worst enemies (critics) are the ones you love the most. As the Billy Joel song says, they "love you just the way you are". They are used to you being a certain way… doing certain things… that make you compatible with their plans, their goals, their dreams.

Hopefully you find yourself in close relationships with mature Christians who want you to find your greatest fulfillment in life and whole-heartedly support your decisions. That would be heaven! But even in well-meaning, loving relationships - even among mature Christians - you might find some resistance to your dreams. We're still living in earthen vessels. None of us are perfect. That's why we need a Savior. And some folks will need Him even more when confronted by your growth and success.

Rather than focusing on visions of their own, family members and close friends may try to meddle with your dreams or cause you to second-guess them. Because they are close, they may feel they have a license to criticize or make a joke of your goals. These "attacks" may not come as full frontal assaults on your "fruit" (accomplishments). Rather, insecurity will cause others to undermine you in small ways. Taken individually, these attacks may seem trivial. However, allowed to remain unchecked, they can undo your success over time.

Nip the insecurity in the bud by understanding the fears of those closest to you. Pray for them. Address issues individually as they arise. Don't wait for your relational challenges to fester or self-remedy. Confront each situation in a spirit of love and reconciliation while remaining true to your vision.

Be aware that some attacks on your fruit will be directly tied to your productivity. As the trappings of success starts coming your way become observant. Those once tied to you at the hip may display jealousy, envy, hostility or anger. Don't be dismayed!

If relationships fall away because you are true to the vision God has given you, chances are they were never meant to be. Although some may draw away from the new, improved you, you must not let their character issues sabotage your quest to become your highest self. Your fruitfulness grows through faithfulness to the vision. That kind of steadfastness will draw attention for sure.

Soon you'll be inspiring many others to seek their own transformation breakthroughs. Even relationships that were challenged initially may be repaired over time. They may desire to join your transformational journey and run the race beside you. Be a trail blazer with no regrets! In the end, it's between you and God. No matter what criticism comes your way, press forward! Be true to your God-given vision or you'll be destined to become a part of another's vision for life.

> *What then shall we say to [all] this? If God is for us, who [can be] against us? [Who can be our foe, if God is on our side?]*
>
> Romans 8:31
>
> Amplified Bible

A WORK IN PROGRESS REQUIRES PROGRESS

The olive tree is most susceptible to the olive fly when deprived of water. When poorly nourished, the crop will become erratic, bearing a heavy crop one year and putting forth not even a blossom the next.

Your "fruit" has an identical susceptibility to that of the olive tree: the fruit is susceptible when it's deprived of water and nourishment. Just as water is the most basic necessity for the survival of your physical life, the Life spring of living water from Christ is essential to sustain your spiritual growth and protect your abundance.

> *...Whoever drinks of the water that I give him will never thirst again; but the water that I give him will become in him a well of water springing up to eternal life.*

John 4:14

World English Bible

Eternal life in God's kingdom is the highest goal of humanity. Yet, in your devotion to God, you cannot make the mistake of being so heavenly minded that you're no earthly good. When you begin to work on the "here and now" person you are, you - like me - will easily recognize that you are not yet fit to rule and reign in God's domain. You are a work in progress. Your lifetime is a time of preparation in kingdom living.

That means you never "arrive". Your transformation is on-going. The work you do proves your faith you possess in God's plan for you.

> *Dear brothers, what's the use of saying that you have faith and are Christians if you aren't proving it by helping others? Will that kind of faith save anyone? If you have a friend who is in need of food and clothing, and you say to him, "Well, good-bye and God bless you; stay warm and eat hearty," and then don't give him clothes or food, what good does that do?*

> *So you see, it isn't enough just to have faith. You must also do good to prove that you have it. Faith that doesn't show itself by good works is no faith at all—it is dead and useless. But someone may well argue, "You say the way to God is*

by faith alone, plus nothing; well, I say that good works are important too, for without good works you can't prove whether you have faith or not; but anyone can see that I have faith by the way I act."

Are there still some among you who hold that "only believing" is enough? Believing in one God? Well, remember that the demons believe this too—so strongly that they tremble in terror! Fool! When will you ever learn that "believing" is useless without doing what God wants you to? Faith that does not result in good deeds is not real faith.

James 2:14-20
Living Bible

We are saved by grace alone unto good works. Your priority, then, should be to conform to the image of Christ - do the work to develop His character - that His love and light might be seen by all who come in contact with you.

For once you were darkness, but now in the Lord you are light. Live as children of light – for the fruit of the light is found in all that is good and right and true. Try to find out what is pleasing to the Lord.

Ephesians 5:8 -10
NRSV Catholic Edition

ACCENTUATE THE POSITIVE

The following suggestions will help you get a firm footing on your transformational path. First things first: Here are some practical steps for nourishing your mind, sustaining your fruitfulness, and protecting your abundance.

Begin to recognize and separate yourself from negative input. Developing a positive attitude begins by distancing yourself from negative environments that challenge your ability to have a breakthrough or achieve your goals. The land of "NO"- where pessimism abounds, criticism runs rampant, and old failures are replayed before you- hinder you as surely as being deprived of air. Identify and eliminate your negative influences: social media forums/blogs/rants, literature filled with vulgarities and themes glorifying immorality, news coverage steeped in conflict, films that are not uplifting or that portray an anti-Biblical world-view, music with salacious or demeaning lyrics, pals who entice/influence you to partake of sinful activities, family members who drag you into the emotional turmoil they are unwilling to resolve, work associates spreading gossip, etc. You get the picture. If you wouldn't read it, say it, watch it, listen to it or act it out in front of Jesus, eliminate it. Negative begets negative.

The thieves of virtue won't bother you in areas where they know you are unshakable; but they'll test your resolve if you are not diligent. Keep your eyes on your goals and off your critics. Flee negativity! Center yourself in a healthy environment which consists of positive people, uplifting activities, and inspirational materials. Speak words of praise and gratitude. They are food for life and health to the body.

Pleasant words are like a honeycomb: they drip sweet food for life and bring health to the body.

Proverbs 16:24

The Voice

If who you are is determined by what you think, and what you think results in what you do, there's no time like now to Plan and Plant for tomorrow's harvest. Accentuate the Positive! Eliminate the Negative. Success is up to YOU!

> *Roll your works upon the Lord [commit and trust them wholly to Him; He will cause your thoughts to become agreeable with His will, and] so shall your plans be established and succeed.*
>
> Proverbs 16:3
>
> Amplified Bible

Before proceeding view your ten year goals. Write Personal Reflections on the space below. Concerning potential enemies, who might deter you from reaching your goals - God's plan for your life. Then move on to the **Olive Tree's Inventory of Assets and Liabilities where your God given gifts will begin to help you know God's plan for your life..**

Reflections:

Reinforce your experience and learning by viewing the artistic video for lesson 3 at:
https://www.articlesoftransformation.com/beamazing/

Be Amazing...

Record your vision and inscribe it on tablets, that the one who reads it may run. For the vision is yet for the appointed time; it hastens toward the goal, and it will not fail. Though it tarries, wait for it; for it will certainly come, it will not delay.

Habakkuk 2:2-3

CHAPTER FOUR

The Olive Tree: Personal Inventory

Moving to the letter I in OLIVE, it is time to take INVENTORY.
Pruning is a highly judicious art. It protects the health of the tree by permitting greater circulation of air; for the olive tree is wind pollinated. The cutting away of live branches may seem foolish, even wasteful, when assessing the tree s abundant productivity in past seasons. Yet this severe act will revitalize an aged tree, compensate for root loss, and promote desirable blossom formation for the coming season.

This example from nature of resolutely pressing toward your vision despite challenges was mirrored in Jesus' purposeful journey to the cross.

> ***Now when the time was almost come for Jesus to be received up [to heaven], He steadfastly and determinedly set His face to go to Jerusalem.***

Luke 9:51
Amplified Bible

Knowing that He would face certain death, Jesus, nonetheless resolved to finish the path to Resurrection. Although His intermediate prospects pointed to pain, and even death, He endured all for the joy set before Him. Like the olive tree, our live branches must be pruned to bear good fruit.

Inventory in retail business is the most dreaded time of year. Every item must be accounted for. So it is in life. This is where you have the opportunity to test your self-honesty. No matter how trivial it may seem, you must give an accounting of all your assets and liabilities. Do not dread this exercise; it will set you free! I promise!

Author, motivational speaker, and ultra long distance runner, Stan Cottrell has run across many countries and has met the peoples of the world face to face: the man in the street to heads of state. After a life lived on an international scope, he made this keen observation of mankind: "Objectivity is a myth. Everything we judge is based on our developed perceptions and opinions." I concur.

When taking inventory, strive to be as objective as possible. When you have finished, you may choose to share your list with a trusted advisor who knows you well enough to assess your findings. This is not the time to share it on social media because once you put it on the Internet it lives forever. You do not want your introspection to become water-cooler conversation. Be serious enough about your life's goals and your chosen path to hold it close to your heart. Go to your Personal Discovery Journal to the Assets and Liabilities exercise. Set aside enough time to accurately and honestly take personal inventory. Do this in the quiet of your home, office or personal retreat without distraction of electronics, phones, or other intrusions. Do not feel like you must complete this exercise in one sitting. Even if you only have a few minutes at a time, list one item. Dwell on it – even if only briefly. Resume the exercise when the next opportunity for solitude presents itself. Plan this time into your schedule as soon as possible.

Do not be alarmed if your list of liabilities is longer than your assets at first glance. Most people think they have a longer list of liabilities than assets. The point of this exercise is honest evaluation for the purpose of eliminating weaknesses and turning them into strengths. Realize that you need time and a plan to change. Some areas may take a year or even longer to alter.

> *The master pruner must know the individual needs of each tree in the grove. With the exactness of a sculptor's skillful hand, he prunes each specimen, taking into consideration the tree's age, health, limb support and penetration of sunlight.*

Your Heavenly Father knows what you need before you even ask.

SACRIFICE NOW TO REAP A HARVEST IN DUE SEASON

Pruning is a highly judicious art. God promised Joseph that he would be a great leader and that his brothers would bow before him. As a youth, Joseph lacked maturity to keep that promise to himself resulting in the resentment of his siblings which led to him eventually being sold into slavery by them. Despite his circumstances, Joseph believed God.

As a servant to Potiphar, Joseph rose through the ranks to become a respected advisor until Potiphar's wife attempted to seduce him. When rejected, she accused him of taking liberties which resulted in his imprisonment. Yet, he still held fast to God's promise.

During Joseph's imprisonment, he was called on to interpret the dreams of the Pharaoh when all the soothsayers had failed. Impressed with Joseph's gift, the Pharaoh restored him to a position of honor, eventually elevating him to the position of Pharaoh's second-in-command. Joseph's spiritual insight saved the Egyptians and indeed brought his starving brothers bowing before him begging for help.

Joseph's trials built character. He grew from an immature dreamer into a wise ruler. Without the pruning he endured with great patience, he would never have been restored to his father's embrace nor realized God's plan for his life.

What is impossible with men is possible with God.

Luke 18:27

Amplified Bible

Pruning live and productive branches from the tree (your life) may be painful as it was for Joseph, but in the eyes of God, and in time, pruning will result in a greater harvest. Many years may pass until reaping a mature crop… your desired vision.

Perhaps a part of your life that has been very productive has been "pruned". It can be very upsetting and bewildering to see this part of your life end. Yet, many times this pruning results in even greater growth and a heavier yield in the future. Pruning cultivates better growth patterns; realize that a new direction may be necessary to achieve your long term goals.

Cutting away liabilities permits greater circulation of air; that is, the pollination of your mind and heart can more easily occur flooding you with positive ideas and altering your path.

Pruning dead wood (weaknesses) serves to strengthen other areas and values of your life. Pruning allows light to reach the inner most part of the tree. Likewise, spiritual pruning – allowing the Holy Spirit to remove the hindrances and non-productive things in your life – allows the Son of God to nourish the inner depths of our hearts.

NO PAIN, NO GAIN
That which appears destitute in the fall will surely prosper for years to come through the master pruner's acts of vision.

The first time I met Anthony Clark was in a maximum security prison in San Quentin, California. He was bench pressing 400 lbs like it was warm up amidst hundreds of hardened criminals while I videotaped the event with 2000 convicts surrounding us; no guards, no guns, no kidding. His record, bench pressing 800 lbs reverse grip, among other successes, gave him the title, The World's Strongest Man. He wore a T-shirt that day with the saying in very large print on the back, **NO PAIN… NO GAIN!** His life story is one of pain to gain. A skinny abused kid bought a Sears set of weights and turned a frightful start in life to one of extraordinary achievement.

It took time, pain, persistence, tenancy, blindness to his nay-Sayers and vision to accomplish his goals. In time he achieved success and great notoriety which he used for God's glory visiting prisons and speaking to young kids about hope and what it takes to weather the storm to accomplish God's plan for their lives. He became a master at his craft and helped shape (prune) many young lives. His message of hope comes from the depth of pain most of us will never experience. He became a very close friend and his words still echo in my ear hear on his answering machine, **"NEVER GIVE UP".** His life was cut short but his legacy lives on. As we read the words concerning the journey of transformation…

At this time, complete the Personal Discovery Exercise on the following pages. Add Personal Reflections before proceeding to the next chapter of *The Articles of Transformation.*

The Articles of Transformation **Personal Discovery Exercise**
Assets/Strengths

Skills and abilities: Talent and knowledge

_____

_____

_____

_____

_____

_____

_____

_____

_____

_____

Character attributes: Mental and ethical traits

_____

_____

_____

_____

_____

_____

_____

_____

_____

_____

These unique traits will help you understand what God has in store for you. Some people discover His plan late in life. Keep the faith!

Liabilities/Weaknesses

Lack of desired skills and abilities (Talent and knowledge)

_____

_____

_____

_____

_____

_____

Lack of character attributes (Mental and ethical traits)

_____

_____

_____

_____

_____

_____

These traits will illuminate what you are not suited for. You're one step closer!

Reinforce your experience and learning by viewing the artistic video for lesson 4 at:

https://www.articlesoftransformation.com/beamazing/

Be Amazing...

Your are uniquely gifted by God!
Begin to discover God's gifts and Plan!

CHAPTER FIVE

The Olive Tree: Value of Your Beliefs

V in the acronym OLIVE represents VALUE of your beliefs.
The following portion of The Ancient Olive Tree contains a vital
character principle.

> *What wisdom requires the olive tree to experience the
> cold and chilling winter in order to blossom and bring forth
> fruit in season?*

Beliefs are what enable, empower, limit or even cripple you. They are
the inner workings of your mind and heart that say "I can do this" or
"I cannot do that"; "I am this" or "It is impossible for me to be...". The
most important principle for transformation that leads to increased
productivity is this: **YOU ARE WHAT YOU BELIEVE.**

It is important that you understand that the processing of words and thoughts over great periods of your life turn into core beliefs. Those deeply held beliefs are what empower or limit you. In a sense, beliefs are what you really think about yourself. It is important to realize that your beliefs and faith determine whether you achieve most of your goals. Faith is your ability to believe you have something (a goal or a vision) when, in fact, you have not yet attained it.

> *For this reason I am telling you, whatever you ask for in prayer, believe (trust and be confident) that it is granted to you, and you will [get it].*
>
> Mark 11:24
> Amplified Bible

Note the words, "*trust and be confident*". That is what belief is. No wavering. In your mind and heart you have it. Consequently, your faith and belief sustains and carries you to the point where you actually possess what you desire or have accomplished your goal or vision.

You are not born with a set of beliefs; they have been developed from your first breath until today. Your environment and shared experiences develop the value of your belief system. Your belief patterns are the by-product of the intensity and length of your life lessons.

The following is an example of the power of belief. When a flea is placed in a jar with a lid on it, the flea will jump and hit its head enough times so that it develops a learned limitation. Soon he will not jump high enough to feel that limiting lid. If the lid is removed after that period of conditioning, the flea will not even attempt to jump out. It will only jump to the height of "learned-limitation" and no higher. The real amazing thing is that their offspring will also have the same learned limitation as their parents. Wow!

We are like the little flea in many ways. We develop mental limitations that dictate our actions. We, like the poor defeated flea, seek the safety of our "comfort zone". Our beliefs set the boundaries that empower or limit our actions. When we stray outside our comfort zone, we feel uncomfortable, fearful or insecure; we soon retreat into our programmed limits.

EXPANDING THE BOUNDARIES WITH POSITIVE BELIEF

I have strength for all things in Christ who empowers me [I am ready for anything and equal to anything through Him who infuses inner strength into me; I am self-sufficient in Christ's sufficiency].

Philippians 4:13

Amplified Bible

You have... You can... You are... Not because of your human effort but because of your dependence on Christ's strength and power.

All you saints! Sing your hearts out to GOD! Thank him to his face! He gets angry once in a while, but across a lifetime there is only love. The nights of crying your eyes out give way to days of laughter.

Psalm 30:5

The Message

Just as the olive tree must experience the chilling winter to even blossom and bring forth fruit in season, we also must experience trials to produce. Trials are for our strengthening. Willingly pay the price. Olive trees in the tropics produce no fruit. If our lives are lukewarm and event-less, we tend to produce the same: a lackluster, nonproductive and non-inspiring character. Our beliefs, developed over time, and tempered by uncomfortable, stretching experiences, hold the promise of the sweetest fruit.

A TRUTH CAN TAKE HOLD AND GROW ANY TIME IN LIFE

Although many fruit trees require either much or little water to flourish, the olive tree will tolerate six months of drought followed by an abundance of water without destructive consequence.

Many of us spend half a lifetime without water... the Truth. Yet, when we receive God's life-changing principles, we gladly drink all that is given and flourish. Although chilling experiences are stern tutors, they very often develop character… if we allow it.

> *And even though Jesus was God's Son, he had to learn from experience what it was like to obey when obeying meant suffering.*
>
> Hebrews 5:8
> Living Bible

The definition of a disciple is "a student under discipline". To be Christ's disciple, we must expect and accept the cold experiences and trials of life. Learn from the painful experiences. Adapt these words from the musical "Carousel" as an exhortation to persevere knowing that God is on your side.

Walk on through the wind,
Walk on through the rain,
Tho' your dreams be tossed and blown
Walk on, walk on
With hope in your heart
And you'll never walk alone...

Like Joseph, develop wisdom from harsh experiences in life; you will blossom and bear fruit in due season. Believe that these experiences are ordered for your strengthening. Willingly accept the tough times as gifts of grace which are given for your strengthening and which will result in a strong, productive belief system.

Even when walking through the dark valley of death
I will not be afraid, for you are close beside me,
guarding, guiding all the way.

Psalm 23:4

Living Bible

A MOST IMPORTANT TO LEARN FROM THE OLIVE TREE

Desirable olives do not come from seedlings; they come from grafting branches of unquestionable quality into young trees which have shown themselves strong.

Desirable olives do not come from seedlings; they come from grafting branches of unquestionable quality into young trees which have shown themselves strong.

Without the grafting process, the olive tree will never realize its full potential. We are no different. All of us require assistance from someone whose merits are beyond our own. If there is one truth I have come to know, it is this: Successful people do not accomplish great success by themselves.

One common thread exists in most successful people: they have mentors. Until we realize we are lacking… insufficient… impoverished without the Grace of God, we can never know what it is to be complete in Him.

> *You don't need a telescope, a microscope, or a horoscope to realize the fullness of Christ, and the emptiness of the universe without him. When you come to him, that fullness comes together for you, too. His power extends over everything.*
>
> Colossians 2:10
> The Message

There is a book titled "**Beware of the Naked Man Who Offers You His Coat**." The title alone should serve as a warning to you. Seek the mentorship of a known commodity… a person of integrity. Accept the mentorship of doers, not talkers. To accomplish your vision, select those to work beside you who have even greater strengths than you. Pride will tell you "do it yourself"; fear will tell you, "the strong and talented will take from you."

But ask yourself this: What is it that you think they are going to take that they don't already have? Push beyond fear and intimidation to reap the rewards of inspiration and experience. You must choose to be vulnerable in order to receive benefits from the strong. More importantly, you must yield to the greatest source of all, God our loving Father. Graft in God's words and allow the Holy Spirit to bring them to life in you.

Eliminate deceptive and limiting beliefs. Move in faith with the certainty that you CAN accomplish what you have set out to do. Trust in and rely on to the Source of life to establish your belief system.

Oh, the joys of those who do not follow evil men's advice, who do not hang around with sinners, scoffing at the things of God. But they delight in doing everything God wants them to, and day and night are always meditating on his laws and thinking about ways to follow him more closely. They are like trees along a riverbank bearing luscious fruit each season without fail. Their leaves shall never wither, and all they do shall prosper.

Psalm 1:1-3

Living Bible

At this time, complete the Personal Discovery Exercise in this section: The Value of Your Beliefs. List some of your obvious beliefs. This exercise will help you determine the **VALUE** of your beliefs and assist you in expanding your perceived limitations/boundaries. You will quickly notice what beliefs are really limiting development in certain areas of your life. Add Personal Reflections before proceeding to the next chapter of The Articles of Transformation.

Personal Reflections:

The Articles of Transformation Personal Discovery Exercise

How you view yourself is the result of your beliefs. Describe your beliefs below:

(I am, I can, etc: **Positive Statements Only**

_____

_____

_____

_____

_____

_____

_____

_____

_____

(I am not, I can't, etc: **Negative Statements Only**

_____

_____

_____

_____

_____

_____

_____

_____

_____

Meditate on the source of your beliefs. Where you have listed a negative "flip the script". Transform it into a positive affirmation and inscribe it in your private journal. Remember *Your words become your thoughts; your thoughts become your beliefs; your beliefs limit or empower your actions!* Be like Joseph and turn the negative into a positive, depending on God to bring it to pass.

PAIN VERY OFTEN DEVELOPS CHARACTER!

And not only that, but we also rejoice in our afflictions, because we know that affliction produces endurance, endurance produces proven character, and proven character produces hope.
Romans 5:3-4
HCSB

**Reinforce your experience and learning by viewing
the artistic video for lesson 5 at:**
https://www.articlesoftransformation.com/beamazing/

Be Amazing...

Expand your positive beliefs!
Anything is possible for him who believes.

Mark 9:23

CHAPTER SIX

The Olive Tree: Envision Your Future

The letter "E" in OLIVE stands for ENVISION and EXPECT the future with EMPOWERED beliefs.

Harvesters look forward to the well-earned reward of their diligent planning, planting, and pruning. When autumn delivers fruit in shades of deep green to a straw yellow or cherry red, harvesting begins. Without fail, the fruit must be gathered before it turns black and before the frost can halt its peak perfection.

See yourself as prosperous and successful, having already achieved your goals and vision. See with the eye of faith to achieve the most important goals you desire.

The visionary attributes of the great men and women of faith in the 11th chapter of Hebrews are prototypes of lives well-lived. Abel, Enoch, Noah, Abraham, Sarah, Isaac, Jacob, Joseph, Moses, Rahab, Gideon, Barak, Samson, Jephthah, David, Samuel and the prophets held fast to their vision with great faith:

The fundamental fact of existence is that this trust in God, this faith, is the firm foundation under everything that makes life worth living. It's our handle on what we can't see. The act of faith is what distinguished our ancestors, set them above the crowd…

Each one of these people of faith died not yet having in hand what was promised, but still believing. How did they do it? They saw it way off in the distance, waved their greeting, and accepted the fact that they were transients in this world. People who live this way make it plain that they are looking for their true home. If they were homesick for the old country, they could have gone back any time they wanted. But they were after a far better country than that— heaven country. You can see why God is so proud of them, and has a City waiting for them…

> *Not one of these people, even though their lives of faith were exemplary, got their hands on what was promised. God had a better plan for us: that their faith and our faith would come together to make one completed whole, their lives of faith not complete apart from ours.*
>
> Hebrews 11:1-2, 13-16, 39-40
> The Message

The faithfulness of those who did not yet achieve in this life time, empowers us not to give up on completing that which they began. The Church was built on the blood of martyrs. That's an unpopular message today. American culture expects an "easy button" quick-fix for everything.

Yet, around the world in this 21st century, more persecution and martyrdom are taking place than at the Church's dawning. A Christ-culture recognizes that true success is not measured in the immediate but rather in the eternal and is measured in the faithfulness to the heavenly vision rather than temporal success.

> **For what does it profit a man to gain the whole world, and forfeit his soul?**
>
> Mark 8:36
>
> NASB

We must not lose heart when delays, detours or even death interrupts our journey. We know that those who endure to the end will see an eternal reward.

Whether your goal is to build a business, finish college or find a mate/have a family, remember that though they are positive goals, they are fleeting. Your transformation into the image of Christ is the ultimate goal. Set your sights on things which bring you fruitfulness in this age and the one to come.

Begin your journey toward that goal by envisioning yourself as strong of heart, fearless, a person of vision and action, one who makes quality decisions and applies discipline to the weighty matters of life. *Envision and Expect* growth.

One cannot help but reflect on the past year when there was little rain and much concern. Yet, the dreams of those planned, planted and pruned have brought forth a bountiful yield. Rehearse these virtues in your inner person by envisioning yourself in the context of Scripture and expecting the outcome promised in God's Word. Read the following aloud substituting the personal pronoun in brackets to fully comprehend the depth of God's promise for you.

So, what do you think? With God on our side like this, how can we [I] lose? If God didn't hesitate to put everything on the line for us [ME], embracing our [MY] condition and exposing himself to the worst by sending his own Son, is there anything else he wouldn't gladly and freely do for us [ME]? And who would dare tangle with God by messing with one of God's chosen? Who would dare even to point a finger? The One who died for us [ME] —who was raised to life for us [ME]!—is in the presence of God at this very moment sticking up for us [ME]. Do you think anyone is going to be able to drive a wedge between us [ME] and Christ's love for us [ME]? There is no way! Not trouble, not hard times, not hatred, not hunger, not homelessness, not bullying threats, not backstabbing, not even the worst sins listed in Scripture:

> *They kill us in cold blood because they hate you.*
> *We're sitting ducks; they pick us off one by one.*
> *None of this fazes us [ME] because Jesus loves us [ME].*
> *I'm absolutely convinced that nothing—nothing living or*
> *dead, angelic or demonic, today or tomorrow, high or low,*
> *thinkable or unthinkable—absolutely nothing can get*
> *between us [ME] and God's love because of the way that*
> *Jesus our Master has embraced us [ME].*

Romans 8:31-39

The Message

Now complete Personal Discovery Exercise. Take the time to really think about your vision and expectations/goals for your future. Remember God knows the plans He has for you.

Seek first the Kingdom of Heaven for your life. All you can imagine will be yours. Be a shinning drop of light in the sea of mediocrity... Be Amazing!

The Articles of Transformation **Personal Discovery Exercise**

List how you ENVISION yourself as 3 years from today.

_____

_____

_____

_____

_____

_____

_____

_____

_____

List your personal EXPECTATIONS for your transformed self 3 years from today:

_____

_____

_____

_____

_____

_____

_____

_____

_____

Vision is powerful. Envision and Expect!

What Vision has God planted in your heart that stirs passion and gives you purpose? Begin to develop a plan for reaching that purpose by writing down critical steps to be made to achieve it below. Be patient.

_____

_____

_____

_____

_____

_____

_____

_____

_____

_____

Personal Reflections:

Reinforce your experience and learning by viewing the artistic video for lesson 5 & 6 at:

https://www.articlesoftransformation.com/beamazing/

Be Amazing...

You are amazing... Believe it!
You are now empowered and
have begun to be and achieve
all that God has planned for you!

CHAPTER SEVEN

The Transforming Power of Words

Excerpts from Chapter 21 in The Articles of Transformation book

So much of how we live is determined by what we speak: good or bad. No matter what you believe, if you say something long enough it will become a part of your inner beliefs. Your words reveal what you believe in your heart. What you believe, you will become.

It is impossible for a good tree to produce bad fruit – as impossible as it is for a bad tree to produce good fruit. Do not men know what a tree is by its fruit? You cannot pick figs from briars, or gather a bunch of grapes from the blackberry bush! A good man produces good things from the good stored up in his heart, and a bad man produces evil things from his own stores of evil. For a man's words will always express what has been treasured in his heart.

Luke 6: 43-45

J.B. Phillips New Testament

So here's what I want you to do, God helping you: Take your everyday, ordinary life—sleeping, eating, going-to-work, and walking-around life—and place it before God as an offering. Embracing what God does for you is the best thing you can do for Him. Don't become so well-adjusted to your culture that you fit into it without even thinking. Instead, fix your attention on God. You'll be changed from the inside out. Readily recognize what he wants from you, and quickly respond to it. Unlike the culture around you, always dragging you down to its level of immaturity, God brings the best out of you, develops well-formed maturity in you.

Romans 12:1-2
The Message

BE TRANSFORMED BY THE RENEWAL OF YOUR MIND

A transformed mind results when an informed mind accepts and submits to the teachings and disciplines outlined in Scripture. The first discipline is to learn about God from His Word. It is excellent to listen to great messages about God and to read and listen to materials which help you grow in faith, but, there will never be anyone or anything that will bring about the transformation you desire that can equal with an in depth and daily study of the Bible.

Work hard so God can say to you, 'Well done.' Be a good workman, one who does not need to be ashamed when God examines your work. Know what his Word says and means.

2 Timothy 2:15
Living Bible

Before you read your Bible, pray. Ask the Holy Spirit to bring the words to life in you… to reveal their purpose for your personal

102

journey. Allow Him to speak to you and be your guide and mentor. Your Personal Discovery Journal is a good companion during your times of reading and meditation. Jot down insights, favorite verses, and inspirations to reflect on. Make them apart of your affirmations and prayers.

When you become a deliberate and faithful student of Scripture, you can expect to gain the wisdom, knowledge and understanding that lead to success in every area of your life. Be disciplined to know what God says: be a true disciple of Scripture by patterning your words and actions after the Living Word, Jesus Christ. Transform your life by agreeing wholeheartedly with God's Word from your lips to your lifestyle.

> *Summing it all up, friends, I'd say you'll do best by filling your minds and meditating on things true, noble, reputable, authentic, compelling, gracious—the best, not the worst; the beautiful, not the ugly; things to praise, not things to curse. Put into practice what you learned from me, what you heard and saw and realized. Do that, and God, who makes everything work together, will work you into his most excellent harmonies.*

Philippians 4:8

The Message

AFFIRMING TRUTH

You won't have to search long to find motivational speakers, self-help counselors, gurus, and religious figures presenting various takes on meditation, contemplation, the merits of thinking positive, and the power of intention. Rarely do they give credit to God for these activities as ordained practices for communing with Him.

Remember the secret to discovering God's plan for your life and achieving personal goals is ...

What you hear, you think...
What you think, you believe...
What you believe, you become!

The contents of this book is based on the powerful scripture God has provided us for spiritual transformation in the book of Romans;

> **Do not be conformed to this age, but be transformed by the renewing of your mind, so that you may discern what is the good, pleasing, and perfect will of God.**
>
> Romans 12:2

AFFIRMATIONS FOR TRANSFORMATION

Being transformed by the renewing of your mind is the secret!

> *An affirmation is a solemn declaration which describes who you are (by faith i.e. the person you will be once you have achieved your personal goal.) It is not a statement of who you will be but who you are in the future.*

Examples of an affirmation:

I am able to speak in front of any size audience without one bit of fear. I prepare and I am fearless when speaking in front of people.

I never procrastinate. I am always on time for meetings by being 15 minutes early. I am never late.

I never use any fowl language. I do not curse, use profanities, or vulgarities. I have learned to express myself with artistically descriptive verse. I never curse. I never use any fowl language.

I never make excuses. I take full responsibility for everything I encounter or situation I place myself in even if it is not my fault. I never make excuses.

No personal will power is required. Only the commitment to repeat your affirmations for 30 days, 3 times a day and once out loud before you go to bed. You will be amazed how you become your words.

Your Words will Become Your Thoughts,
Your Thoughts will Become Your Beliefs,
Your Beliefs will Empower You.

Personalize God's Word for powerful affirmations.
Example:

> **God didn't give us a spirit that makes us weak and fearful. He gave us a spirit that gives us power and love. It helps us control ourselves.**
>
> 2 Timothy 1:7

Change to:

> God didn't give **me** a spirit that makes **me** weak and fearful. He gave **me** a spirit that gives **me** power and love. It helps **me** control myself.

You will find an extensive list of life changing affirmations on the following pages. *Pick only one easy affirmation*, personalize it, and repeat if for the next 30 days. Your life will change!

This is the most powerful exercise you will perform in your life!
Be Amazing!

Adversity: I am not afraid because God is at my side! He has given His angels charge over me. (Luke 4:10)

Associations: I walk in the counsel of the righteous friends of God. (Psalms 1:1)

Becoming Centered: I am level-headed and centered because I have the mind of Christ. (Philippians 2:5)

Charitable Endeavors: God loves a cheerful giver and I love to give! (2 Corinthians 9:7)

Compassion: I have a great feeling of warmth and compassion for other people knowing we are all God's children. (Ephesians 4:32; 1 Peter 3:8)

Confidence: I do all things through Christ who strengthens me! (Philippians 4:13)

Confrontation: Confrontation comes easy for me because I know it is the least painful route to a successful relationship... even if it makes the other person uncomfortable initially. (Proverbs 27:6)

Creativity: I am a very creative person. I quickly and easily come up with the right solution and act to implement the idea. (1 Peter 4:10; Proverbs 18:16)

Decisions: I quickly and easily make decisions without wavering. Then, I comfortably implement those decisions, constantly moving toward my desired goals. (Psalms 37:5)

Direction: I seek God first in all things, and I am sure He will always direct my path. (Proverbs 3:6)

Discipline of my words: I am careful with my words, not to speak quickly but to count the cost of what I say. I realize every word I speak I will account for; so, I am convinced of and speak words of life, encouragement and love. (Psalms 19:14; Matthew 12:36)

Energy: I have an abundant supply of energy for anything I want to do.

Enjoying Health: A merry heart does good like a medicine: I choose to be happy. (Proverbs 17:22)

Enthusiasm: I love what I am doing and my enthusiasm is contagious. (Colossians 3:23)

Fear: God has not given me a spirit of fear! (2 Timothy 1:7)

Flexibility: I move in new directions very comfortably and easily. I am very comfortable and relaxed when plans change. (Ecclesiastes 3:1; Philippians 1:27)

Focus: I am single of mind and in purpose; I do not get swayed by the confusion massing around me. (Luke 9:51)

Goals: I constantly set up new goals for greater use of my potential. I help make them a reality by daily seeing myself through the eye of faith already performing at the goal level of effectiveness. (Psalms 127:1; Proverbs 16:3)

Goals: I make a list of things to do each morning and complete them in their order of importance no matter how easy or difficult. (Psalms 20:4)

Health: I know that for every hour I exercise, I will live two hours longer so I enjoy the physical activity that extends my life. (Proverbs 3:6)

Honesty: I am honest with myself, and therefore I am comfortable being honest with other people. Lies are not a part of my way of life. (Proverbs 12:22; 2 Corinthians 8:21)

Health: By His stripes we were healed. Healing is mine for the asking because of Jesus' sacrifice. (Isaiah 53:5; 1 Peter 2:24)

Life's Foundation: I am assured of success because I have built my life on the foundation laid out in Scripture that leads to blessing. I cannot fail! (Psalms 127:1)

Memory: I quickly and easily recall information stored in my memory. The Holy Spirit will bring all things to my remembrance. (John 14:26)

Order: I resist confusion and heighten my productivity by utilizing organizational skills and putting things away when I am finished. (1 Corinthians 14:40)

Promises: My "yes" is "yes", my "no" is "no". I rarely make promises but when I do I keep them. (Matthew 5:37)

Positive Associations: I take counsel from the Godly. I choose my companions wisely. (Psalms 1:1)

Purpose: God has a plan for me, for good and not for evil. I continually seek His plans for my life to be a light and salt because I am a part of the kingdom of God. (Jeremiah 29:11; Matthew 5:13-16)

Promises: I rarely make promises; but when I do, I always do what I say I'm going to do. I do not make promises I can't keep. (Ecclesiastes 5:4)

Priorities: I always make sure to "keep the main thing the main thing". (Matthew 6:33; Romans 12:2; Luke 12:34; John 14:15)

Public Speaking: I am very relaxed and comfortable speaking before a group of people. I know my purpose for speaking and communicate my ideas in a clear, understandable form with conviction. I have no fear of public speaking. (Colossians 4:6; Jeremiah 1:4-10)

Reading: I read with great speed and with excellent comprehension. I have the mind of Christ. (1 Corinthians 2:16)

Relaxation: I relax quickly and easily whenever I wish to do so. God keeps me in perfect peace for my mind is stayed on Him. God is my perfect peace. (Isaiah 26:3)

Response to Pressure: I respond positively to pressure. It brings out the very best in me. I am very relaxed and comfortable under pressure. I never let pressure turn to stress. (1 Peter 5:7; Matthew 11:28-30)

Salvation: NOTHING can separate me from the love of God. (Romans 8:31-19)

Success: I am very successful in the things I undertake. I finish what I start. (1 Corinthians 9:24) (Isaiah 40:31)

Strength: I am a child of God and I am accepted in the beloved. I am more than a conqueror through Christ. (Deuteronomy 33:12; Romans 8:37) Proverbs 15:1)

Tranquility: Because I trust in God, He gives me perfect peace because I trust Him completely. (Isaiah 26:3)

Work Habits: I work hard... I work smart... and I work honestly (right). Therefore prosperity is mine. (1Timothy 5:18; Proverbs 13:4; Proverbs 12:24)

Teacher - Parent: Encouraging my children to accomplish the tasks before them - without excuses - builds character as they realize their discipline leads to achievement and reward. (Proverbs 22:6; 2 Corinthians 10:5)

Victory: No weapon formed against me shall prosper. (Isaiah 54:17)

Worry: The Lord is my Shepherd and loving Father; I shall not worry or want for anything... anything (Psalms 23)

Personalize one of the above affirmations. Write it on a card and repeat your affirmations for 30 days, 3 times a day, and once out loud before you go to bed. You will be amazed how *you become* your words

Your Words will Become Your Thoughts,

Your Thoughts will Become Your Beliefs,

And Your Beliefs will Empower You.

The Final Word and Ultimate Vision: Eternal Life

In the western world, one's ultimate vision to attain eternal life is generally tied to what is described as the Judeo-Christian ethic or religion as defined by the Holy Scripture: the Bible. Before exploring how to actually achieve the ultimate goal of eternal life, let's make sure we're on the same page of understanding: common ground. Consider the following definition of religion as found at *www.dictionary.com.*

Religion: *a set of beliefs concerning the cause, nature, and purpose of the universe, especially when considered as the creation of a superhuman agency or agencies, usually involving devotional and ritual observances, and often containing a moral code governing the conduct of human affairs.*

Although attempting to offer a broad-sweep definition of religion, www. dictionary.com failed to include those who chose disbelief in a specific "god" - or in any God at all - as is the practice of atheists, agnostics and pagans. Those without belief in a guiding force beyond themselves, or those who worship nature or many paths leading to "spirituality", are now included in the religious mainstream. In fact, one of today's most popular bumper stickers promotes the unity of all religions with the slogan "co-exist". Such a "faith' might make a good lyric for John Lennon's imagined world, but in reality, it is an impossible dream. The beliefs and practices of even just the twelve largest religions are at odds on major issues with all faiths but their own. Yet, today's theological discourse has made room along side of orthodox faith and practice for the religion of secularism: Secular religion is *a communal belief system that often rejects or neglects the metaphysical aspects of the supernatural, commonly associated with traditional religion, instead placing typical religious qualities in earthly entities.* (*Wikipedia*).

So what we have under the wide umbrella of **religion** are colliding spiritual world views. Religion's laws, commandments, or guidelines demand observance or obedience from devotees in order that they might obtain right standing in the faith. As with the concept of *karma* (the belief that a person's actions in life will determine their fate in the next life), consequences for non-submission, or lack of obedience to the accepted moral code, is exacted from followers in this life time and the lifetime to come.

The penalties for wrong doing vary in the practice of one religion from another; however; broken laws (sin) exacts a price that must be paid in most cases. Many religious persons spend a lifetime of effort trying to overcome the penalties for their personal short-comings with kind acts, charitable giving, and prayerful pleas for mercy. The burden is a great spiritual weight upon those who try to personally meet the terms of obtaining forgiveness for the magnitude of their sins. Personal good works and adherence to strict standards are their hope of finding justification or worthiness before their "god". And perhaps the worst payment of all is excised from the secularists who look in the mirror each day to face themselves in their weaknesses. They are without hope and have no one to turn to for encouragement of soul or forgiveness of sin.

Only one religion provides its followers with the assurance of saving grace. And, that faith is Christianity. *Webster's Collegiate Dictionary's* first definition of the grace of God is **"unmerited divine assistance given man for his regeneration or sanctification. So grace is "unmerited favor".**

The Amplified Bible, Classic Edition fully fleshes-out biblically what Webster attempted to define. It clearly describes grace as salvation and forgiveness from sin by the unmerited favor (gift of God) through our faith (belief in the vicarious death and resurection) of Jesus Christ.

For it is by free grace (God's unmerited favor) that you are saved (delivered from judgment and made partakers of Christ's salvation) through [your] faith. And this [salvation] is not of yourselves [of your own doing, it came not through your own striving], but it is the gift of God; Not because of works [not the fulfillment of the Law's demands], lest any man should boast. [It is not the result of what anyone can possibly do, so no one can pride himself in it or take glory to himself.]

Jesus Christ is Savior, Redeemer, and the Advocate who personally paid the penalty for all our sins: past, present and future! Jesus Christ bore the penalty for sin upon the cross of Calvary. He gave His sinless life as payment (sacrifice) for all sin that we might obtain or inherit His "sozo" life. *The New Testament Greek Lexicon* lists the use of the word "sozo" 108 times.

Sozo is defined as follows: to save, keep safe and sound, to rescue from danger or destruction

    a. one (from injury or peril)

        1. to save a suffering one (from perishing), i.e. one suffering from disease, to make well, heal, restore to health

        2. to preserve one who is in danger of destruction, to save or rescue

    b. to save in the technical biblical sense

When Jesus said, "**You haven't done this before. Ask, using my name, and you will receive, and you will have abundant joy**" (John 16:24 *New Living Translation*), he was explaining the gift of "sozo": life found in Him alone. He brings forgiveness, eternal salvation, deliverance, healing, and abundant blessings and favor to all who call upon His name and welcome Him into their hearts as Savior and Lord. **To as many as believe on His name and in His vicarious life, death and resurrection, God grants newness of life – a rebirth - which cleanses them from all unrighteousness.**

Does spiritual rebirth make us "perfect"? No. And yet, veiled in His Son's light, His love, His power over sin and death – washed in His blood by faith - we can boldly approach the throne of God as beloved, sinless children. We cease from dread, from labor, from fear of death and enter His eternal kingdom without end by faith alone. That's the Gospel: the **Good News!** Jesus conquered the enemies of our souls and paid the penalty for everything we ever did or will do. So great is His love that He willingly gave His life for you and me that we might live eternally in the peace and glory of His presence.

Prayer to Receive Jesus as Savior and Lord

Lord Jesus, come into my heart. I believe you died for my sins. I ask you to be my Savior and the Lord of my life. Teach me to be like you. Develop your character in me that I might share your love and saving grace with others. I will confess my faith in you before men knowing that you will declare my righteousness before the Heavenly Father. This single act of faith delivers me from the kingdom of darkness to walk in your marvelous light. I am now a new creation; and you have written my name in the Lamb's Book of Life. Thank you that by your grace alone I will live forever.

Come Holy Spirit. Teach me, guide me, anoint me, and empower me to live a life that reflects the same love and grace I have received. Thank you, Lord Jesus, for your amazing sacrifice that has set me free and cleansed me whiter than snow. Thank you Heavenly Father for your divine plan for my life. **Amen.**

For it is by believing in your heart that you are made right with God, and it is by openly declaring your faith that you are saved.

Romans 10:9-10 New Living Translation

Blessed [fortunate, prosperous, and favored by God] is the man who does not walk in the counsel of the wicked [following their advice and example],Nor stand in the path of sinners, or sit [down to rest] in the seat of scoffers (ridiculers). But his delight is in the law of the LORD, and on His law [His precepts and teachings] he [habitually] meditates day and night. And he will be like a tree firmly planted [and fed] by streams of water, which yields its fruit in its season; Its leaf does not wither; and in whatever he does, he prospers [and comes to maturity].

Psalms 1:1-3 Amplified Bible

His Amazing Grace
Has Already Made You Amazing!

Thank you for making me so wonderfully complex! It is amazing to think about. Your workmanship is marvelous—and how well I know it. You were there while I was being formed in utter seclusion! You saw me before I was born and scheduled each day of my life before I began to breathe. Every day was recorded in your book!

Psalms 139:14-16

Living Bible

Be Amazing! Learn how from... the Ancient Olive Tree
is the first lesson in *The Articles of Transformation* series.
Accompanying videos at: www.articlesoftransformation.com/beamazing.

Available on Amazon or directly from Visible Light Ministries

Domenic and Charlie Fusco are available for speaking engagements, workshops, and retreats. Direct all inquiries to:

Visible Light Ministries
PO Box 4200
Sanford Fl 32772
407-341-6999

www.visiblelight.org
www.articlesoftransformation.com

Made in the USA
Columbia, SC
28 May 2019